THIS JOURNAL BELONGS TO

A PRAYER JOURNAL

DON'T WORRY

ABOUT ANYTHING; INSTEAD,

PRAY

ABOUT EVERYTHING

MY PRAYER JOURNAL

DAILY PRAYER

LORD, HEIGHTEN MY SPIRITUAL SENSES

TO SEE THAT WHICH IS NOT VISIBLE,

HEAR THAT WHICH IS NOT AUDIBLE,

SENSE THAT WHICH IS NOT TANGIBLE,

BELIEVE THAT WHICH IS UNBELIEVABLE.

TEACH ME TO SORT THROUGH

THE NOISES OF THIS WORLD,

TO HEAR AND DISCERN YOUR POWERFUL,

WONDERFUL, PURE, PRECIOUS VOICE.

WRITE A LOVE LETTER TO GOD

SPIRITUAL NOTES TO MYSELF

PRAISE HIM FOR TRUTH

SPIRITUAL NOTES TO MYSELF

THANK HIM FOR A BLESSING

SPIRITUAL NOTES TO MYSELF

REWRITE YOUR FAVORITE SCRIPTURE IN A PRAYER

SPIRITUAL NOTES TO MYSELF

WRITE A LIST OF THINGS YOU ARE THANKFUL FOR AND PRAY THE LIST TO GOD

SPIRITUAL NOTES TO MYSELF

WRITE A PRAY ASKING FOR HELP TO FORGET THE FORMER THINGS AND STRENGTH TO MOVE PAST ANY AREAS OF STRUGGLE.

SPIRITUAL NOTES TO MYSELF

WRITE OUT A PRAYER IN AN AREA YOU ARE STRUGGLING IN ASK THE LORD TO HELP YOU OVERCOME IT.

SPIRITUAL NOTES TO MYSELF

GIVE YOURSELVES COMPLETELY TO GOD

SPIRITUAL NOTES TO MYSELF

PRAY FOR YOUR LOVED ONES

SPIRITUAL NOTES TO MYSELF

PRAY FOR YOUR ENEMIES TO FORGIVE

SPIRITUAL NOTES TO MYSELF

WRITE OUT A PRAYER FOR YOUR SOUL

SPIRITUAL NOTES TO MYSELF

PRAY FOR THE WORLD (COMMUNITY & COUNTRY)

SPIRITUAL NOTES TO MYSELF

ASK GOD FOR WISDOM FOR WHAT YOU ARE FACING

SPIRITUAL NOTES TO MYSELF

WRITE A LETTER TO GOD SHARING WHAT IS ON YOUR HEART

SPIRITUAL NOTES TO MYSELF

MAKE A LIST OF YOUR NEEDS AND PRAY OVER THE LIST

SPIRITUAL NOTES TO MYSELF

PRAY FOR THOSE YOU KNOW WHO ARE NOT SAVED

SPIRITUAL NOTES TO MYSELF

PRAY FOR YOUR PURPOSE, YOUR CALLING

SPIRITUAL NOTES TO MYSELF

WRITE OUT THE LORD'S PRAYER

SPIRITUAL NOTES TO MYSELF

PRAY ABOUT HOW YOU CAN BE A TOOL IN

SPIRITUAL NOTES TO MYSELFGODS HAND

ANSWERED PRAYERS

SPIRITUAL NOTES TO MYSELF

ASK

AND IT WILL BE GIVEN TO YOU;

SEEK

AND YOU WILL FIND;

KNOCK

AND IT WILL BE OPENED TO YOU.

A PRAYER JOURNAL

Made in the USA
Monee, IL
27 January 2022

90096992R00030